You are already moving through noise.

This book is about getting above it.

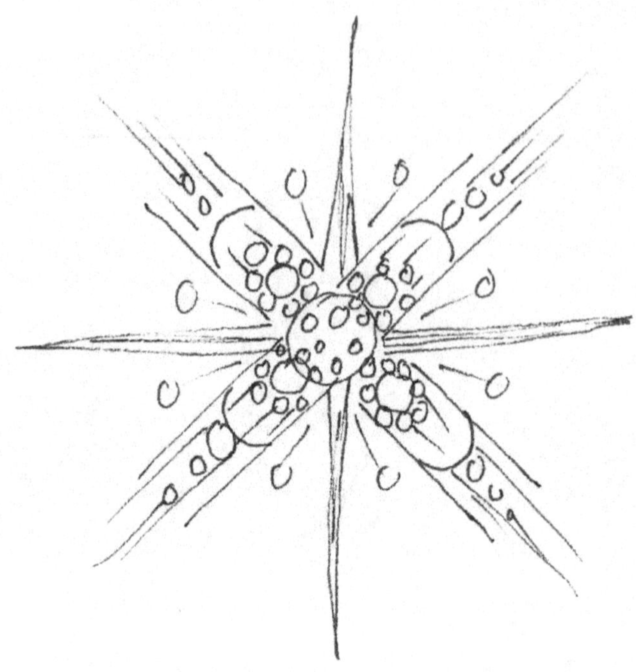

First Edition, 2026.
BioMind Superpowers Books.
ISBN-13: 978-1-949214-99-4

You Know More Than You Think
A Five-Book Series

Book Four
Above the Noise
Explorations in Living What You Know

Elly Flippen

A BIOMIND SUPERPOWERS BOOK
PUBLISHED BY

Swann-Ryder Productions, LLC

DISCLAIMER

This book is provided for informational, educational, and experiential purposes only. It is not intended as medical, psychological, psychiatric, therapeutic, legal, or scientific advice, nor should it be used as a substitute for professional diagnosis, treatment, or consultation.

The author is affiliated with Swann-Ryder Productions, LLC, which holds certain copyrights and related intellectual property rights to the published and unpublished writings and artwork of Ingo Swann. This book may reference, quote, or discuss his published material for educational and contextual purposes. All interpretations, analyses, applications, and contemporary extensions presented herein are solely those of the author.

Nothing in this book should be interpreted as representing official positions of any scientific, governmental, institutional, or research organization. References to perception research, anomalous experience, or non-ordinary awareness are included for historical, educational, and phenomenological exploration.

This work does not claim to prove, validate, or guarantee the existence of paranormal, psychic, extrasensory, or supernatural abilities, nor does it present such phenomena as scientifically established fact.

Individual experiences will vary. No guarantees are made regarding outcomes, results, insights, or personal transformation.

Readers are responsible for their own engagement with the material and for their physical, emotional, and psychological well-being. Individuals with a history of trauma, dissociation, significant mental health conditions, neurological or cardiovascular concerns, or other medical conditions should consult a qualified healthcare professional before engaging in any practices described.

The practices described in this book are voluntary exercises intended for personal exploration and should be approached with discretion and self-awareness.

While reasonable efforts have been made to ensure the accuracy of the information presented, the author and Swann-Ryder Productions, LLC assume no responsibility for errors or omissions and make no warranties regarding the completeness, reliability, or applicability of the material.

By choosing to engage with this book, the reader accepts responsibility for its use and for any decisions or actions arising from the material presented.

READER GUIDANCE

The following guidance is offered to support safe, grounded, and thoughtful engagement with the practices and explorations presented in this book.

Readers are encouraged to:

> Move at a pace that feels appropriate and sustainable.
> Modify, pause, or discontinue any practice that creates discomfort, distress, or instability.
> Seek qualified professional support when encountering intense emotional, psychological, or perceptual experiences.

The material in this book is not intended to replace sound judgment, professional care, or responsible engagement with daily life, relationships, and decision-making.

These practices are offered as invitations to explore awareness and perceptual literacy, not as doctrines of belief, systems of authority, or substitutes for medical, psychological, or therapeutic care.

Your consent, grounding, safety, and discernment are foundational to your engagement with the material presented here.

TABLE OF CONTENTS

HOW TO APPROACH THIS BOOK

This volume continues the exploration developed in the previous books. It is not material to master, but material to move through with attention.

By this point, the question is no longer how meaning forms, but how your orientation is maintained while meaning moves through experience.

This book examines what allows your awareness to remain navigated rather than absorbed, and what allows what you perceive to remain usable rather than overwhelming.

Understanding here develops through lived engagement. Some sections may feel immediately practical; others may seem understated at first.

This is natural. Integration at this stage often follows experience rather than preceding it.

The pages that follow are designed to orient your attention within real situations: how perception, emotion, and interpretation interact while events are unfolding.

If something does not become clear immediately, allow it to remain open. Recognition often develops through participation rather than explanation.

Restraint reveals more than force.

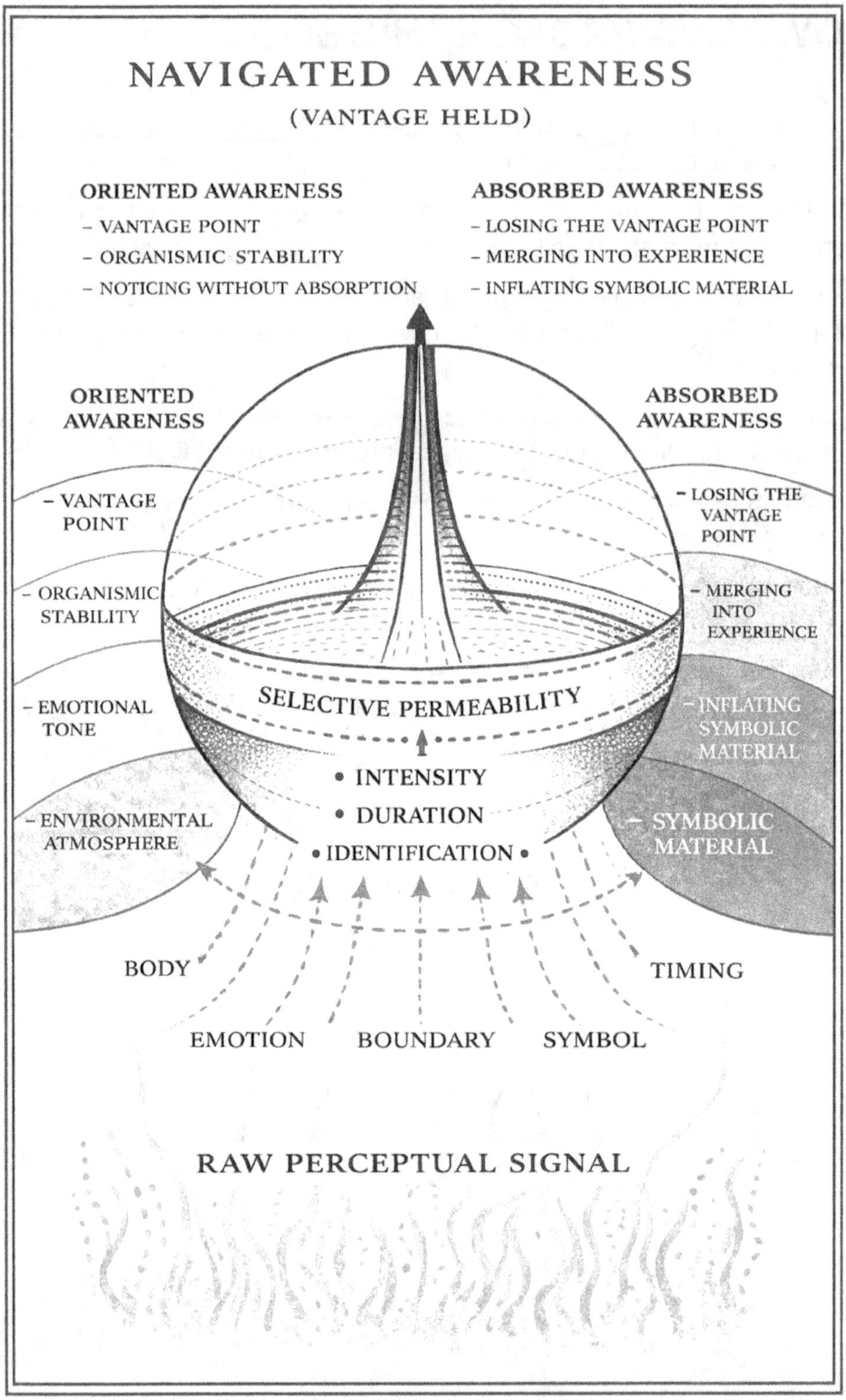

NAVIGATED AWARENESS
(VANTAGE HELD)

ORIENTED AWARENESS
- VANTAGE POINT
- ORGANISMIC STABILITY
- NOTICING WITHOUT ABSORPTION

ABSORBED AWARENESS
- LOSING THE VANTAGE POINT
- MERGING INTO EXPERIENCE
- INFLATING SYMBOLIC MATERIAL

ORIENTED
AWARENESS

ABSORBED
AWARENESS

- VANTAGE
POINT

- ORGANISMIC
STABILITY

- EMOTIONAL
TONE

- ENVIRONMENTAL
ATMOSPHERE

- LOSING THE
VANTAGE
POINT

- MERGING
INTO
EXPERIENCE

- INFLATING
SYMBOLIC
MATERIAL

- SYMBOLIC
MATERIAL

SELECTIVE PERMEABILITY

- INTENSITY
- DURATION
- IDENTIFICATION

BODY

TIMING

EMOTION   BOUNDARY   SYMBOL

RAW PERCEPTUAL SIGNAL

Reading as Navigation

The preceding diagram illustrates navigated awareness and absorbed awareness.

It is not a model to decode in advance. It is a structural reference that becomes clearer through use.

The diagram maps:

> the difference between vantage held and vantage lost
> how selective permeability regulates exchange
> how intensity, duration, and identification shape experience
> how symbolic and emotional material can inflate when orientation collapses
> how organismic stability preserves discernment

It is not a problem to solve.

It is a structure to recognize as you move through lived situations.

Return to it when:

> your attention feels pulled inward
> symbolic material becomes compelling
> your emotional tone overrides orientation
> perception feels intrusive rather than usable

This book is not about becoming more open.

It is about becoming more regulated.

Reading as Experience

This book shifts emphasis from inner exploration to navigation in motion.

Each chapter refines how your system operates in real situations: in relationship, decision, and changing context.

Recognition may occur during interaction rather than during structured practice. Clarity may follow action rather than precede it.

The aim is ongoing orientation rather than momentary insight.

The explorations that appear throughout the book are not techniques to master or states to sustain.

They function as temporary vantage points that make regulatory dynamics visible.

Suggested Pacing

A steady rhythm supports integration. Speed offers no advantage.

Chapters may be entered non-sequentially when circumstances require it, but depth increases when the developmental arc is respected.

Consistency stabilizes perception.

Intensity destabilizes it.

Repetition in this volume strengthens regulation. With recurrence you may notice:

> earlier detection of overwhelm
> quicker recovery of vantage
> reduced symbolic inflation
> more stable boundary differentiation

Stability develops through use.

Familiarity builds trust in your own system.

If effort increases, pause.

If intensity rises, regulate before expanding.

GETTING READY

Before beginning, orient to a simple principle:

> Expansion without regulation leads to absorption.
> Regulation allows expansion without collapse.

Nothing in this book asks you to suppress organismic intelligence. The emphasis here is maintaining your orientation while information moves through your awareness.

As what you perceive encompasses more, the task is not to control what appears, but to remain positioned in relation to it.

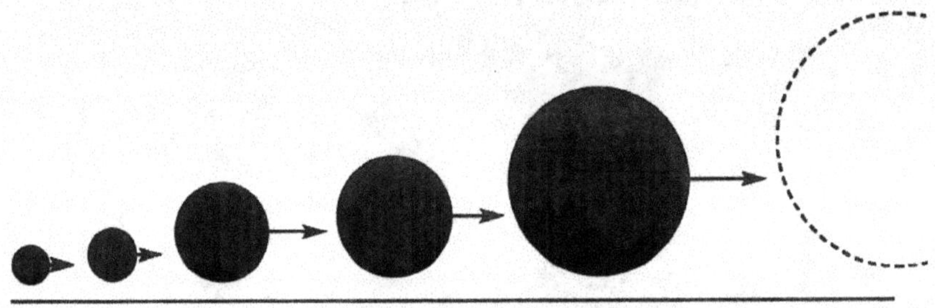

DEVELOPMENT

Approaching the Explorations

The explorations in this book are not models to adopt. They are structured situations that make regulatory dynamics visible in real time.

Their relevance may not be obvious at first.

Often it becomes clear later, when a reaction softens sooner than expected, when a boundary holds under pressure, or when urgency no longer dictates movement.

When that happens, return to the material.

The explorations are not techniques to perfect.

They are experiments in maintaining a vantage point while the perceptual process moves.

Go slowly through them. There is no advantage to speed. Recognition often develops after experience rather than during it.

Each exploration also includes *What to Watch For* and reflection questions.

> *What to Watch For* points are not predictions or guarantees. They are orientation cues, examples of how shifts may appear, so they are less likely to be overlooked.
> *Reflection* questions are not meant to be answered correctly. They are invitations to remain with your experience long enough for it to clarify. If other questions arise, you are encouraged to follow them as well.

Once an exploration concludes, allow your system to return to its natural baseline. Integration develops through recognition in lived situations rather than through maintaining a particular condition.

If something feels effortful, confusing, or destabilizing, pause and return to basic orientation:

> breath
> posture
> boundary
> connection with the room
> ordinary spatial reference

These simple adjustments help restore a course-plotting point, allowing your awareness to remain navigable rather than overwhelming.

Brief reset practices are outlined in the Appendix.

They are available whenever needed and serve as supports for restoring orientation rather than corrective measures.

Regulation restores clarity faster than force.

Pauses & Reflection Spaces

Throughout the book, you will encounter brief pauses labeled:

⟩ Pause. Check orientation.
⟩ What you're noticing.

These are not prompts to analyze or explain. They are moments to assess whether orientation is intact while experience is unfolding.

You will also find spaces for notes or sketches. These are not assignments to complete or conclusions to reach. They are places for experience to land while it is still organizing.

Not everything registers as language. Some information may appear as:

⟩ sensation
⟩ spatial awareness
⟩ image or symbolic fragment
⟩ movement or directional pull
⟩ a shift in proportion or readiness

A few words, a brief phrase, a line, or a simple sketch is often enough. Writing or drawing can help stabilize early impressions without forcing interpretation.

Not every pause produces a clear answer. Silence is a valid response. Neutrality is information. The absence of urgency is also information.

Key Takeaway

Not everything you notice will immediately make sense.

Ambiguity does not necessarily indicate confusion. It often signals that meaning has not yet organized. When information is still forming, interpretation cannot yet be stable.

What feels unfinished may simply be in motion.

Allow it time.

More is always occurring within organismic perception than reaches passive awareness. Subtle signals register alongside ordinary seeing and hearing, often before the intellect intervenes.

When you remains grounded in your orientation, timing, and boundary, that information becomes usable rather than overwhelming.

In this book, clarity comes not from intensity, but from navigation.

The word ambiguous comes from a root meaning to wander.

It does not originally describe confusion, but movement; meaning that has not yet settled.

In common usage, ambiguity refers both to what is unclear and to what can be understood in more than one way.

These are not separate conditions.

When perception has not yet taken form, meaning has not yet organized.

What is indistinct naturally allows multiple readings—not because it is wrong, but because it is unfinished.

Ambiguity and amorphousness are linked in this way.

Where form has not yet emerged, interpretation cannot yet be stable.

— Adapted from Ingo Swann,
Awareness and Perception vs Status of Individual "Realities"

LIVING WHAT YOU KNOW

ORGANISMIC INTELLIGENCE IN MOTION

The Navigating Experience

By now, you have not been learning how to become someone else.

You have been recognizing how to relate more deliberately to what is already occurring.

Book One invited you to notice what your system was revealing.

Book Two helped you stabilize so perceptual information could become usable.

Book Three clarified how meaning forms and how perception organizes before interpretation.

This book asks a different question.

Once perception becomes clearer, the question is no longer:

Can I sense this?

It becomes:

> How do I live from what I sense?
> How do I move and decide while perception continues to unfold?
> How do I remain myself while awareness widens?

That question is not about what is available to be aware of.

It is about navigation.

Navigation means remaining positioned while experience moves. Information may arise through body, emotion, symbol, or timing, but awareness does not collapse into any single signal.

When orientation is maintained, perception remains usable.

When orientation collapses, even accurate signals can become overwhelming or distorted.

This book explores how awareness remains navigable in real situations: in conversation, decision-making, and changing environments.

You are not being asked to chase extraordinary experiences.

You are learning how to live from organismic intelligence as it operates in ordinary life.

What Navigation Requires

In Book Four, navigation depends on three capacities that must operate together:

1. **Holding Orientation**

    The capacity to remain aware of experience without becoming absorbed in it.

2. **Selective Permeability**

    What you allow in, what you hold, and what you release, so information remains usable rather than overwhelming.

3. **Contextual Discernment**

    Recognizing when perception is shaped by relational, environmental, or situational context rather than direct registration.

    These are not techniques to perform.

Together, these capacities allow perception to remain integrated rather than fragmented.

Up to now, you may have explored what appeared to be independent skills:

⟩ sensing your body and perceptual boundaries
⟩ reading emotional tone
⟩ recognizing symbolic impressions
⟩ tracking distortion and noise
⟩ noticing shifts in rooms, groups, and timing

In lived experience, these do not operate as autonomous channels. They belong to a single living system: organismic intelligence.

This book explores how that system functions in motion: how information, context, and response organize together as you move through your life.

18 I Holding Orientation
The Vantage Point

Opening Invitation

There is a part of you that:

⟩ senses
⟩ feels
⟩ analyzes
⟩ reacts

And there is a mode of active awareness that notices all of this without being pulled into it. You may already recognize it:

⟩ the moment you observe a reaction instead of becoming it
⟩ the moment you sense someone's mood without absorbing it
⟩ the steadiness that remains present during disruption
⟩ the quiet calm behind thought
⟩ the clarity that sees without effort

This is not a separate self, and not a deeper aspect of consciousness.

It is a functional vantage point within awareness: the capacity to remain oriented while sensation, emotion, and thought move.

When this vantage point is not available, information is easily shaped by:

⟩ emotional charge
⟩ desire or fear
⟩ symbolic drift
⟩ others' emotional influence
⟩ cognitive overlay
⟩ compression of complex data

When it is present, what you perceive becomes:

⟩ steadier
⟩ cleaner
⟩ less reactive
⟩ more sustainable over time

This chapter explores how your orientation stabilizes naturally, and why this vantage point is essential for maintaining clarity as what you are aware of begins to encompass more.

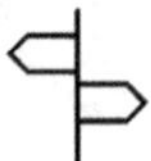

What Is Holding Orientation?

In Book Three, you explored how perception organizes across multiple reference frames (personal, relational, environmental, collective, and symbolic) and how your perceptual-awareness interface functions as the space between signal and interpretation.

Holding orientation builds on that foundation.

It is the capacity to remain aware of experience without becoming absorbed in it.

When this orientation is present, active awareness tends to be:

> emotionally neutral
> perceptually distinct
> embodied
> steady
> receptive
> less reactive

This orientation does not interpret or assume.

It notices.

It does not identify with experience; it remains oriented while experience unfolds.

At your perceptual-awareness interface with the world (the space between you and what you perceive) maintaining orientation prevents collapse.

Emotion, symbolic imagery, and relational influence can be recorded without immediately becoming identity, belief, or reaction.

This does not make perception perfect.

It makes distortion visible earlier in the sequence.

This is not detachment or dissociation.

It is presence (grounded, awake, and embodied) within the interface itself.

Pause. Check resonance.

Pause. Check resonance.

Why Holding Orientation Matters

When your orientation is unstable:

> emotion colors information
> symbolic impressions inflate
> boundaries soften
> relational influence blurs
> attention becomes entangled
> perceptual coherence becomes harder to maintain

When your orientation is stable:

> signals can be tracked without immediate interpretation
> symbols remain symbolic
> emotions move without taking over
> boundaries remain clearer
> complex information stays organized longer
> what you perceive remains steadier under intensity

Holding orientation functions as an anchor, allowing your awareness to enlarge without loss of clarity.

Three Gates to Orientation

You do not need all three.

Any one of them can help you ease into this vantage point.

Each gate shifts your orientation in a slightly different way:

1. **Stillness**

   Allowing sensory activity to resolve so the deep background of your awareness becomes noticeable.

2. **Neutrality**

   Releasing preference and emotional pull so experience can be observed without leaning toward or away.

3. **Perspective Shift**

   Moving from immersion in experience to recognizing it as something occurring within your awareness.

These are not techniques to perform in sequence; rather they are discrete ways of identifying the same functional vantage point.

Pause. Check resonance.

19

Pause. Check resonance.

You may find one gate more natural than the others. Use whichever one restores steadiness in you most easily in the moment.

When your vantage point steadies, you begin to notice that your awareness itself moves through different depths.

If we observe the workings of our own minds, we notice that they contain different classes (almost species) of mental activity. Beyond the ordinary activities of waking thought, there are deeper strata or levels within the mind. We already recognize which of these are superficial and which are profound. We sense ourselves moving through them when we meditate or fall asleep and rising back through them as we approach wakefulness.

— Adapted from Ingo Swann, *Everybody's Guide to Natural ESP*

Notes.

Debates about what the senses are can continue indefinitely.

A more useful question is what they do.

Consider this before beginning the material that follows.

Pause. Check resonance.

Gate 1: Stillness
The Quiet Behind Sensation

Stillness is one of the simplest ways to recognize the vantage point of awareness.

When sensory activity relaxes slightly, the background noticing that is always present becomes easier to detect.

This exploration does not create awareness. It simply makes the vantage from which noticing occurs more apparent.

Steps
1. Sit comfortably.
2. Notice your breath for about 10 seconds.
3. Feel the weight of your body on its support.
4. Let your attention inhabit your torso.
5. Ask: *What is noticing this?*
6. Do not look for an answer.
7. Allow your attention to rest with the quiet awareness present behind sensation, breath, and thought.

That understated noticing is the vantage point itself.

It is not something you observe.

Instead, it is the place from which observation occurs.

It is not an object, but an orientation within attention.

Gate 2: Neutrality
Releasing Preference & Emotional Pull

Neutrality is not coldness.

It is equanimity: the ability to notice experience without leaning toward it or pushing it away.

When preference relaxes, your awareness naturally relaxes into a steadier vantage point.

This does not remove emotion.

It allows emotion to be present without immediately shaping perception.

Steps

1. Bring to mind something mildly emotional.
2. Notice where it registers in the body.
3. Ask: *Can this be observed without becoming it?*
4. Allow the emotion to move within awareness.
5. Let any charge soften slightly, without forcing change.

As preference loosens, the vantage point becomes easier to maintain.

From this orientation, information can reach your awareness without being immediately shaped by attraction or resistance.

Emotion remains present, but it no longer directs attention automatically.

Pause. Check resonance.

Gate 3: Perspective Shift
From Immersion to Witnessing

This gate works by shifting orientation, not by altering the experience itself.

Instead of changing what is occurring, you change where your awareness is positioned in relation to it.

Steps

1. Notice a current experience:
    → sensation
    → emotion
    → symbolic image
    → a general sense of activation or tone
2. Acknowledge it as something occurring, not something you are.
3. Allow a small sense of internal space around it.
4. Let your attention rest in what is noticing.

The experience does not need to change, only your relationship to it does.

When your orientation shifts in this way, your awareness naturally returns to the vantage point from which experience can be observed.

From that position, information remains usable rather than absorbing.

Signs a Vantage Point Is Present

These are indicators, not requirements.

Orientation can appear in diverse ways, and not all of these will arise every time.

1. **Inner Space**

    Thoughts and sensations move without crowding one another. You may notice a sense that awareness has room, allowing experience to unfold without pressure or compression.

2. **Smoothing of Experience**

    Sharp edges, spikes, or contractions begin to soften or organize themselves. What previously felt jagged or reactive may start to move more fluidly.

3. **Untroubled Clarity**

    Perception becomes clearer and more neutral, without urgency. Things can be noticed directly without the immediate need to interpret or resolve them.

4. **Decoupled Awareness**

    Experience is noticed rather than inhabited. You remain present without being pulled into it, often accompanied by a quiet sense of observing from within awareness itself.

5. **Lack of Demand**

    Nothing presses for immediate action, interpretation, or conclusion. What is occurring can unfold without the sense that something must be decided right away.

When these qualities appear, orientation is often already established.

Pause. Check resonance.

Orientation & Broader Awareness

When your experience is processed reactively, it tends to become:

> inflated
> over-personalized
> confusing
> emotionally charged

When it is received from a stable orientation, it remains:

> more coherent
> symbolically clean
> steadier
> meaningful without urgency

From this orientation, complexity can unfold without collapse. You awareness widens while perceptual coherence remains intact.

Orientation in Relationships

When your orientation is stable:

> emotion can be sensed without absorption
> openness does not require merging
> relational dynamics register without loss of center
> responsiveness replaces reactivity

Relational perception becomes more ethical, well-defined, and sustainable over time.

This is not withdrawal. It is ethical presence.

It develops not through disengagement, but through remaining oriented while fully present.

Pause. Check resonance.

Pause. Check resonance.

An Example of Perception Held in Orientation

The following passage comes from waking dream work Ingo undertook with Dr. Gerald (Jerry) N. Epstein (1935–2019), a psychiatrist and early pioneer in mind-body medicine. Dr. Epstein's work explored the relationship between imagery, embodiment, and healing, emphasizing the mind's influence on physiological organization. This excerpt is offered not for interpretation, but as an illustration of posture:

Notice:

> the lack of urgency
> the absence of identification
> the observational tone
> the clarity without effort

> Instead of tunnels and all that, I found myself at some position in space above the monastery, which was situated on dark-green hills. In the distance were snowy mountains. There was a pink-orange light over everything. I did not have a "body" of any kind and had vision in all directions at once, like 360 degrees.

Having established this, Jerry asked me to go down into the monastery, at which point I encountered the gateman. It was he who had been with me in the night dream. We went through some doors and into a large receiving room. It was tall, with colorful banners and wall hangings.

Jerry asked to find out why I was there, and the gateman told me that this monastery belonged to me. The attendants were just keeping it until I would return to be there again.

On the right side of the entry hall was a narrow flight of stairs going upwards. There were twenty-four of them, and they were made of gold. At the top was a buddha-like figure, a seated statue—Hindoo in some way. It was of gold, and in its head were little holes out of which laser-like beams came, radiating in all directions.

While I was looking at this, the statue opened in half and inside was a sort of womb of pink and orange-gold-yellow light. I was being invited into this Buddha—in a sense, to become it and reassume the powers I once had.

33

EXPLORATION 18.1: The 20-Second Drop
A Rapid Re-Orientation

Objective

To re-orient your system quickly in everyday situations.

Setup

Sit or stand where you are.

Steps

1. Notice your breath for about 5 seconds.
2. Notice the space around your body.
3. Gently shift your attention to what is noticing the breath and the surrounding space.
4. Allow your attention to rest there briefly, without effort.

What to Watch For

> a faint settling or easing
> your breath becoming less driven
> a sense of space around experience
> reduced urgency or pressure

Reflection

↻ What, if anything, shifted when you changed orientation?
↻ Did clarity appear without needing to do anything more?
↻ Did the experience itself change, or did your relationship to it change?
↻ Was there a brief sense of space between you and what you were noticing?
↻ Did any reduction in urgency or emotional pull occur?
↻ How quickly did the shift happen once your attention moved to the noticing itself?

EXPLORATION 18.2: Observing Emotion Without Becoming It
Emotional Clarity

Objective

To notice emotion clearly without suppressing it or being carried by it.

Setup

Sit in a way that feels stable. Let your breathing continue naturally.

Steps

1. Bring to mind a mild emotion from earlier in the day.
2. Notice how it registers in your body.
3. Re-orient the vantage point of your awareness (using any of the gates from this chapter).
4. Allow the emotion to be present while it is noticed from this orientation of awareness.
5. Note the difference between:
   → This feeling is happening.
   → I am noticing this feeling happening.

What to Watch For

⟩ emotional charge softening on its own
⟩ more space around the feeling
⟩ the emotion moving rather than staying fixed
⟩ your body holding the feeling without needing to resolve it immediately
⟩ your awareness remaining steady while the emotion shifts or fades

Reflection

↺ What allowed the emotion to be noticed clearly, if anything did?
↺ How did observing the feeling differ from trying to manage or change it?
↺ Did the emotion itself change, or did your relationship to it change?
↺ Was there a moment when the feeling was present without fully defining your experience?
↺ Did noticing the emotion from a stable orientation affect its intensity or movement?

What you're noticing.

EXPLORATION 18.3: Relational Sensing
Sensing Without Absorbing

Objective

To notice another person's emotional tone while maintaining clarity and self-orientation.

Setup

Rest into your seat and allow your breath to organize on its own.

Steps

1. Place your attention onto another person (in your presence or recalled lightly from memory).
2. Notice any emotional tone or relational signal that registers.
3. Re-orient the vantage point of your awareness (using any of the gates from this chapter).
4. Allow what registers to be noticed without leaning toward it or away from it.
5. Notice how your own sense of center remains present while observing it.

What to Watch For

> clearer differentiation between self and other
> reduced pull to merge or react
> steadier internal boundaries
> your attention feeling simpler or quieter
> your emotional tone registering without immediately becoming personal
> the ability to notice signals without needing to resolve them

Reflection

↻ Did the information feel simpler or less dramatic when observed from this vantage point?
↻ What aspects of the experience clearly remained yours?
↻ Did you notice a distinction between sensing and interpreting?
↻ Did maintaining orientation affect how much emotional pull you felt?
↻ How did the experience change when you stayed centered while observing?

EXPLORATION 18.4: Symbolic Material
Holding Complexity Without Collapse

Objective

To notice symbolic material clearly without inflating it or breaking it down prematurely.

Setup

Take a steady seat. Notice your breath as it is.

Steps

1. Direct your attention to a recent symbolic impression (from a dream, reflection, or new perception).
2. Allow it to be present without interpreting or explaining it.
3. Re-orient the vantage point of your awareness (using any of the gates from this chapter).
4. Notice the symbol as something occurring within your system, rather than something you are inside of.
5. Observe what remains steady and what changes when your attention stays neutral.

What to Watch For

> dramatic or story-like elements softening
> underlying structure, tone, or quality remaining
> less urgency to explain or resolve the symbol
> a sense of increased neutrality or steadiness
> meaning becoming quieter rather than louder
> the symbol appearing simpler when not interpreted

Reflection

↺ What, if anything, persisted when the symbol was only observed?
↺ What changed or faded when interpretation was set aside?
↺ Did the symbol feel different when noticed from a stable orientation?
↺ Were you able to distinguish between the symbol itself and the meaning you might normally assign to it?
↺ Did remaining neutral affect how complex or intense the symbol seemed?

What you're noticing.

**Integration Practice 18
Returning to Orientation**

Several times a day:

1. Pause briefly.
2. Notice what is happening: internally or around you.
3. Re-orient your vantage point of your awareness (using any of the gates from this chapter).
4. Allow any reactivity to soften without forcing it.
5. Hold your orientation from this vantage point for a few breaths.

This is perceptual maturity in practice: the ability to remain present, clear, and responsive without becoming entangled.

Observations.

Closing Thought

Holding orientation is not something you acquire. It is something you remember how to return to.

From this vantage point:

> information organizes
> distortion weakens
> clarity stabilizes

From here, what you perceive becomes steadier, clearer, and easier to live from.

19 | Selective Permeability
Regulating the Awareness Exchange Without Closing

Opening Invitation

As organismic perception comes online, a common misunderstanding arises: that clarity requires openness without limit.

In practice, the opposite is true.

Perceptual maturity depends not on how much what you are aware of expands, but on how selectively it allows information to enter, circulate, and settle.

This chapter explores selective permeability: your system's capacity to regulate the perceptual-awareness interchange process (what becomes meaningful in real time) without shutting it down or allowing it to become overly porous.

Selective permeability is not a belief. It is not a technique, rather it is a biological and perceptual function already operating in you… often unconsciously.

When it functions well:

> what you perceive feels classifiable rather than overwhelming
> information is measured without flooding
> boundaries remain flexible rather than defensive
> what you are aware of stays responsive without becoming absorbed

When it breaks down:

> what you pick up becomes noisy or intrusive
> emotional or symbolic material overwhelms
> relational influence bleeds inward
> your system compensates by closing, hardening, or dissociating

This chapter makes that regulating function visible.

What Selective Permeability Is (& Is Not)

Selective permeability describes how a living system manages exchange.

In biology, a permeable membrane:

> allows nutrients in
> lets waste out
> blocks what would cause harm
> adjusts dynamically to conditions

Your organismic intelligence works the same way.

Selective permeability determines:

> what registers
> how deeply it registers
> how long it stays active
> whether it integrates or overloads

It is not:

> emotional suppression
> skepticism
> control
> detachment
> openness as an identity

It is regulation.

Your perceptual-awareness interface does not need to be wide to be accurate; it needs to be well-regulated.

The Role of Friction in Regulation

In many contemporary environments, information arrives without resistance. Signals are designed to bypass delay, to capture attention immediately, and to remain active. This can create the impression that greater openness leads to greater awareness.

In practice, awareness without friction becomes overexposed.

Small forms of deliberate friction restore regulation:

> pausing before responding
> allowing a signal to register before interpreting
> not reacting at first contact
> choosing when to engage rather than engaging automatically

Friction here does not mean discomfort for its own sake. It means restoring pacing to what you take in. Selective permeability depends on that pacing. Without it, intake exceeds integration. Regulation begins when pacing returns.

Why Information Becomes Unusable Without It

When organismic perception expands without selective permeability, several predictable problems appear:

1. Everything feels meaningful.
2. Emotional tone bleeds into interpretation.
3. Symbolic material inflates.
4. Relational signals overwhelm personal orientation.

Your system may begin to oscillate between over-openness and shutdown. This is not sensitivity. It is loss of regulation.

Selective permeability allows you to:

> receive without absorbing
> sense without merging
> record information without identifying with it

Without it, your system often compensates by:

> intellectualizing
> dismissing perceptual information altogether
> tightening boundaries rigidly
> retreating from relational or symbolic awareness

The solution is not less experience. It is better regulation of engagement.

Pause. Check resonance.

The Three Axes of Perceptual Permeability

Selective permeability allows information to enter your awareness without overwhelming it or being lost. It operates across three interacting axes:

1. Intensity
How much signal is allowed in at once.

⟩ Too much → flooding
⟩ Too little → dullness

Healthy permeability allows graded access, not all-or-nothing openness.

2. Duration
How long information remains active.

Some signals:

⟩ register briefly and pass
⟩ require extended holding
⟩ need time to integrate

Without regulation, signals linger too long or disappear too quickly.

3. Identification
Whether you notice information or become identified with it.

Permeability breaks down when:

⟩ emotion becomes identity
⟩ symbol becomes belief
⟩ relational tone becomes personal truth

Healthy permeability preserves differentiation.

These three axes determine whether information remains usable or becomes overwhelming

Pause. Check resonance.

Healthy Indications of Permeability

When permeability is functioning well, you may notice:

> signals arriving without overwhelming your awareness
> impressions remaining detectable without needing to intensify
> information staying present long enough to organize, then releasing naturally
> emotions or symbols appearing clearly without becoming identity
> relational information registering without pulling you out of your center

The process feels open yet organized, allowing your awareness to remain steady while information moves through it.

When permeability drifts out of alignment, your awareness may become either overwhelmed or constricted.

Common Misalignments

You may recognize that selective permeability is compromised when:

> what you perceive feels intrusive rather than informative
> clarity collapses under social or emotional intensity
> symbolic material becomes dramatic or compelling
> boundaries alternate between porous and rigid
> the vantage point feels unsafe to inhabit

These are not failures. They are signals that regulation must precede expansion.

Regulation restores permeability; permeability restores clarity.

Pause. Check resonance.

EXPLORATION 19.1: Perceptual Gating

Letting Information Be Present Without Entering It

Objective

To experience the difference between noticing and absorbing.

Setup

Take a steady seat. Notice your breath as it is.

Steps

1. Notice a neutral sensation (breath, pressure, sound).
2. Allow it to form fully.
3. Ask: *Can this be noticed without entering me?*
4. Let the sensation remain at the boundary of your attention.
5. Notice the difference between:
   - → registration
   - → absorption

What to Watch For

⟩ increased lucidity with less intensity
⟩ steadier boundaries
⟩ reduced emotional pull

Reflection

↺ When the sensation remained at the boundary of attention how did it differ from when it felt "inside" you?

↺ Did noticing without absorption change the intensity, clarity, or neutrality of the experience?

↺ Was there a sense of effort involved in holding the boundary, or did it organize itself naturally?

↺ How did your breath, posture, or emotional tone respond when absorption was not required?

↺ Did what you were aware of feel more spacious, more stable, or simply quieter?

What you're noticing.

What you're noticing.

EXPLORATION 19.2: The Permeability Dial
Adjusting Without Closing

Objective

To experience permeability as adjustable rather than fixed.

Setup

Adopt a supported posture. Allow your breathing to regulate itself.

Steps

1. Bring your attention to your perceptual boundary.
2. Gently imagine a dial with three settings:
   → narrow
   → balanced
   → wide
3. Shift your attention between them slowly.
4. Notice which setting feels most usable right now.

What to Watch For

⟩ relief when balance is restored
⟩ increased perceptual coherence
⟩ reduced effort

Reflection

↻ Which setting felt most supportive in this moment: narrow, balanced, or wide?
↻ How did your body signal the difference between each setting (breath, posture, tone)?
↻ Did adjusting permeability feel like control, or like allowing the system to self-correct?
↻ What signaled that a setting had gone too far in either direction?
↻ How quickly could you shift once you noticed the need to adjust?

EXPLORATION 19.3: Information Release
Letting Signals Exit Cleanly

Objective

To notice that permeability includes release, not just intake.

Setup

Establish a steady posture. Let your breathing remain unforced.

Steps

1. Recall a signal that lingered too long.
2. Reorient your attention to your body.
3. On an exhale, allow the signal to complete.
4. Do not resolve or interpret it.

What to Watch For

⟩ completion without conclusion
⟩ quieting of attention
⟩ restored neutrality

Reflection

↺ How did the signal change when you allowed it to complete without explanation?
↺ What shifted first as the signal exited (attention, emotional tone, or bodily sensation)?
↺ What was different about release compared to suppressing or analyzing the signal?

**Integration Practice 19
Returning to Orientation**

Throughout the day, ask briefly:

1. Is this signal useful right now?
2. Is it asking to be held or released?
3. Am I noticing, or absorbing?

No answer is required. The question itself is meant as regulation.

Observations.

Closing Thought

Selective permeability is not about protection. It is about usability.

When your perceptual-awareness interchange process can regulate:

> what you perceive stays distinct
> meaning forms gradually
> boundaries remain flexible
> orientation is preserved

A regulated system creates the conditions for coordinated movement.

Once what you perceive is selectively permeable, the question shifts from

What am I allowing in?

to

How do I move coherently while multiple contexts are active at once?

20 I Integrated Navigation
Navigating Perceptual Contexts with Clarity & Stability

Opening Invitation

By now, you've journeyed through how to notice and stabilize:

> your body's internal state
> the perceptual space between people
> the atmosphere of rooms and places
> emotional frequency and tone
> symbolic impressions
> deeper-pattern information beneath immediate awareness
> timeline signals as they begin to register

You've built this map piece by piece.

Perception doesn't change by adding structures. It matures by recognizing how it is already organized.

Integrated perceptual navigation is where these capacities are used together. This is done not as an exercise, but in real life:

> conversations
> decisions
> relationships
> difficult environments
> creative work
> impressions that arrive without explanation

This chapter is about how to remain oriented while multiple perceptual contexts are active at once, without losing your orientation, clarity, or boundary.

Note: Chapter 17 explored how to interpret signals cleanly. This chapter focuses on how to stay oriented while multiple signals arrive at once.

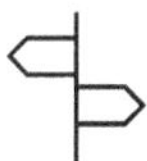

The Four Contexts You Move Through Daily

In Chapter 12, you were introduced to perceptual reference frames: internal orientations that determine what information becomes available, how it is organized, and what registers as meaningful before belief or interpretation takes hold.

Those reference frames operate continuously and simultaneously.

What changes with development is not the frames themselves, but how actively and soundly they are navigated.

In lived experience, these reference frames are encountered as perceptual contexts: the immediate, functional orientations through which your organismic intelligence organizes information in real time.

For clarity and practical use, this chapter works with four operational perceptual contexts, which correspond directly to the reference frames introduced earlier and most directly shape real-time navigation:

1. **The Personal Context**
    (Personal Reference Frame)
    Your body, breath, emotional tone, coherence, and inner state.

2. **The Relational Context**
    (Relational Reference Frame)
    The perceptual space between you and another person: the interaction zone where attention, emotion, and responsiveness meet.

3. **The Environmental Context**
    (Environmental Reference Frame)
    The atmospheric qualities of a room, building, landscape, or natural setting as they register in your system.

4. **The Deep Context**
    (Symbolic / Collective Reference Frames in operation)
    The underlying orientation of your interface, where information organizes as pattern, timing, symbolic impression, and non-linear structure rather than direct sensory detail.

What was previously described as the deep background of perception does not function as an isolated context to move into or out of. It is the organizing backdrop against which different perceptual reference frames become available.

In everyday experience, this background orientation most often becomes noticeable through relational contexts (shared attention, group tone, unspoken coordination) and environmental contexts (the felt history of a place, collective mood, or atmosphere).

When a room's mood is immediately apparent, or when a shift takes shape before interaction begins, your system is already operating against this deeper background.

For this reason, the deep background is not treated here as an additional context alongside the personal, relational, and environmental.

Instead, it is understood as the underlying orientation that allows these contexts (and the deeper patterns they carry) to be registered, organized, and navigated with perceptual coherence.

Integrated perceptual navigation means recognizing, and maintaining perceptual coherence across, these contexts as conditions change:

⟩ which reference frame is currently organizing what you perceive
⟩ how that orientation is influencing experience
⟩ how to re-orient cleanly without blending, overload, or loss of your vantage point

Pause. Check resonance.

63

Pause. Check resonance.

1. The Personal Context

Your baseline. Anchor here first.

The personal context includes:

> body sensation
> emotional tone
> breath rhythm
> grounding
> internal boundary
> capacity (how much experience you can hold without overload)

A simple rule: if your personal context is unstable, everything else becomes unreliable.

Integrated perceptual navigation begins here, through:

> grounding
> holding orientation
> awareness of emotional frequency
> boundary integrity

This context is not something you "enter." It is the reference point from which all other perceptual contexts are sensed and interpreted.

Pause. Check resonance.

2. The Relational Context

The perceptual space where interaction occurs.

Every interaction generates a shared perceptual atmosphere. This space may register as:

> warm or cool
> sharp or soft
> heavy or light
> open or overwhelming
> clear or tangled
> magnetic or resistant

These qualities are not abstract. They are how interaction is sensed before words or interpretation take shape.

The key skill here is simple, but foundational: knowing where your experience ends and another person's begins. This requires:

> regular boundary checks
> maintaining orientation in your vantage point
> awareness of your emotional frequency
> closing or releasing your attention after engagement
> withdrawing your attention when needed

When this context is navigated cleanly, connection remains possible without absorption, and responsiveness does not require self-loss.

Pause. Check resonance.

3. The Environmental Context

How places register in perception.

Rooms and places carry perceptual tone.

Every place registers through qualities such as:

> density
> rhythm
> brightness or dullness
> residue (emotional, social, or historical)
> pressure points: areas where the body tightens without an obvious personal cause

These qualities are not imagined. They are how environments are taken in before you decide what you think or feel about them.

Integrated environmental navigation involves:

> attuning to tone quickly, without analysis
> noticing how your internal state shifts upon entry
> distinguishing environmental tone from your personal emotion
> adjusting your orientation without hardening or withdrawing
> finding internal steadiness even within loud or crowded spaces

This context becomes especially important in complex settings, where clarity depends less on control and more on accurate differentiation.

> *Pause. Check resonance.*

4. The Deep Context

Where meaning registers beneath the immediate perception.

The deep context refers to the mode of perception where information arrives as pattern, timing, and symbolic impression, rather than as direct sensory detail or linear thought. This context includes:

⟩ symbolic cognition
⟩ archetypal tone
⟩ non-local patterning
⟩ timeline sensitivity
⟩ meaning that arrives without language

Information from this context is subtle and powerful, but it remains stable only when the personal context is coherent and grounded.

Integrated navigation here involves:

⟩ remaining embodied while impressions register
⟩ observing without merging or identifying
⟩ distinguishing signal from noise
⟩ allowing meaning to remain symbolic rather than literal
⟩ disengaging cleanly once the process has completed

This context does not replace the others. It adds depth and timing to them, when your orientation is stable.

Pause. Check resonance.

The Art of Navigating Multiple Contexts at Once

Integrated perceptual navigation is the ability to remain centered while simultaneously tracking:

> your body and emotional state
> the tone of the environment
> another person's presence and responsiveness
> impressions registering beneath immediate awareness

...without collapsing into overwhelm, confusion, or self-loss.

This is not about tracking everything at once.

It is about staying oriented while multiple perceptual contexts are active.

The Four-Anchor System

A stability map you can return to at any moment.

These four anchors help maintain perceptual coherence when the range of information you are registering widens.

Think of them as touchpoints you can check in any order:

1. **Body**
   What is your body doing right now?
   (tight, soft, heavy, light, buzzing, settled)

2. **Breath**
   Is your breath moving?
   (high in the chest, low in the belly, shallow, steady, smooth, constricted)

3. **Boundary**
   Where does your attention feel located?
   (close, diffuse, overly wide, contained)

4. **Vantage Point**
   From what internal orientation are you perceiving?
   (reactive identification or a vantage point)

When confusion appears, return to the anchors.

They restore orientation before interpretation begins.

Pause. Check resonance.

Pause. Check resonance.

The Navigation Loop

A real-time sequence usable anywhere.

1. **Notice**
   Receive the raw signal as it registers.
2. **Anchor**
   Return the focus of your attention briefly to your body, breath, boundary, and vantage point.
3. **Differentiate**
   Identify which perceptual context the signal belongs to: personal / relational / environmental / deep.
4. **Interpret**
   Apply the clean meaning-making process (Chapter 17).
5. **Disengage**
   Release your attention and return to your baseline orientation.

This loop prevents entanglement and keeps perceptual information usable in real time.

Differentiating Contexts in the Moment

When multiple impressions overlap, ask:

1. Is this arising from my internal state?
2. Is this registering from another person?
3. Is this coming from the environment or setting?
4. Is this emerging as a pattern, timing shift, or symbolic impression?
5. Or is this simply activation or noise (fatigue, stress, hunger, overstimulation)?

You do not need to answer perfectly.

Over time, patterns become familiar:

> personal signals tend to feel embodied and internal
> relational signals tend to feel as if they occur between people
> environmental signals tend to feel atmospheric or location-based
> deeper signals tend to appear as pattern, timing, or symbolic impression

Differentiation reduces confusion.

Clarity follows naturally.

Pause. Check resonance.

Pause. Check resonance.

EXPLORATION 20.1: The Four-Context Walkthrough
Multiple Perceptual Contexts in Sequence

Objective

To notice the distinct texture of each perceptual context without analysis or interpretation.

Setup

Establish a steady posture. Let your breathing remain unforced.

Steps

1. Bring your attention to your personal context (body sensation, breath, emotional tone).
2. Include the relational context (the sense of connection or responsiveness with someone in your life, even at a distance).
3. Include the environmental context (the atmosphere of the space you are in).
4. Finally, allow your attention to rest in the deep context (the quieter background where impressions register as pattern, symbol, or timing).
5. Move through these slowly. There is no need to hold them all at once.

What to Watch For

> where your attention seems to orient as each context is included
> whether your sense of location, distance, or immediacy shifts
> any changes in your breath, posture, or boundary awareness
> differences in how information registers without naming or interpreting them

Reflection

↻ Which context was easiest to notice?
↻ Which felt more unfamiliar?
↻ Did your sense of boundary or orientation shift as you moved through the sequence?
↻ Did any context feel closer, farther away, or more spacious than the others?
↻ Did the quality of information change as you moved from one context to another?
↻ Were you able to remain oriented while shifting between contexts?

EXPLORATION 20.2: Context Separation in Conversation
Sorting Your Experience From What Is Shared

Objective

To reduce confusion in conversation by recognizing how personal, relational, and environmental contexts register distinctly in experience.

Setup

Sit comfortably. Let your breath move without adjustment.

Steps

1. Recall a recent conversation that stayed with you in some way.
2. In writing, note what you observed in each area:
   → Personal Context: your body sensations and emotional tone.
   → Relational Context: what seemed present in the interaction itself.
   → Environmental Context: the atmosphere of the space.
   → Activation or Noise: anything that felt amplified, residual, or unclear.
3. If helpful, create separate columns (Personal / Relational / Environmental / Activation) and place observations without analysis.
4. The goal is not accuracy, but differentiation.

What to Watch For

〉 where your experience felt blended or difficult to place
〉 whether some sensations or tones appeared before interpretation
〉 whether anything seemed to linger after the interaction ended
〉 how separating contexts changes your sense of clarity or ownership

Reflection

↺ What felt distinctly personal in your experience?
↺ What seemed to belong to the interaction itself rather than to either person individually?
↺ Did anything appear to come from the environment or atmosphere of the setting?
↺ What felt amplified, residual, or difficult to place?
↺ Did separating the contexts reduce any confusion or emotional intensity?

What you're noticing.

What you're noticing.

EXPLORATION 20.3: Navigating Deeper Perceptual Material Without Losing Ground
Staying Oriented While Symbolic Information Is Present

Objective

To notice how symbolic impressions can be held within your system without amplification, urgency, or collapse into narrative.

Setup

Sit in a way that feels stable. Let your breathing continue naturally. The emphasis is on how information is held, not on what appears.

Steps

1. Allow a symbolic impression to be present (image, texture, movement, tone, or fragment of meaning).
2. Bring your attention to physical grounding in your body: your feet, your breath, your spine, and where your body meets its support.
3. Re-orient your attention toward a stable vantage point (using any of the contexts from this chapter).
4. Let your perceptual boundary remain comfortably close and intact.
5. Observe the impression as it is, without pursuing interpretation or explanation.

What to Watch For

> how your body, breath, or boundary responds
> whether your attention stabilizes, shifts, or disperses
> what happens when meaning is not actively pursued
> how the impression organizes (or doesn't) when left unforced

Reflection

↺ What was present when you observed without interpreting?
↺ How did grounding influence your experience of the impression?
↺ What changed when your boundary and observation were maintained together?

EXPLORATION 20.4: Real-Time Navigation Loop
Applying Integrated Orientation in Daily Life

Objective

To familiarize yourself with a repeatable sequence for staying oriented when multiple perceptual contexts are active. You may experiment with this loop during:

> a conversation, a decision, a meeting
> an emotionally charged moment
> a symbolic impression
> a timeline-related signal

Move through the sequence in whatever pacing feels natural:

1. Orient. Briefly recognize your vantage point of awareness before engaging with the experience.
2. Notice. Allow the initial impression to form.
3. Anchor. Reconnect your attention briefly with your body, breath, boundary, and vantage point.
4. Differentiate. Identify which perceptual context the impression seems to belong to (personal, relational, environmental, or deep).
5. Interpret. Apply the clean meaning-making process from Chapter 17, if interpretation is needed.
6. Disengage. Release your attention and return to your baseline orientation.

The loop is not meant to be rigid. It is a reference sequence you can enter or exit as needed.

What to Watch For

> how your orientation changes when anchoring is included
> which steps tend to be overlooked or rushed
> how your interpretation feels when it follows differentiation
> what happens in your system when you disengage deliberately

Reflection

↺ Which part of the sequence felt most stabilizing for you?
↺ Where do you tend to lose orientation: noticing, differentiating, interpreting, or disengaging?
↺ Did beginning with orientation affect how the impression registered?

Integration Practice 20
The Multi-Context Orientation Check

At moments throughout your day, you may pause briefly and notice:

1. What is my personal context doing right now?
2. What is the relational context doing (if I'm with someone)?
3. What is the environmental context doing?
4. Is the deeper background of perception active right now, or relatively quiet?

This is not meant to become constant monitoring or self-surveillance.

It is a simple orientation check (an internal glance) that becomes lighter and less effortful with familiarity. Over time, your recognition can stabilize and occur without deliberate prompting and begin to happen automatically.

Observations.

Closing Thought

Integrated perceptual navigation is not about sensing more.

It is about remaining yourself while sensing more.

When you can:

〉 stay grounded in your personal context
〉 remain stable within relational contexts
〉 register environmental tone without confusion
〉 notice deeper-pattern information without overwhelm…

…information becomes coherent rather than scattered.

From this orientation, you can move through complex emotional, relational, and subtle landscapes with steadiness, discernment, and presence, without losing center, boundary, or clarity.

What follows is not a new capacity, but a synthesis: how these orientations function together as one integrated human perceptual system.

21 | Organismic Intelligence
Distinct Perceptual Functions Operating as One Coherent System

Opening Invitation

Everything you've explored so far:

> sensing space
> feeling presence
> reading emotion
> working with symbols
> navigating perceptual contexts
> noticing timeline signals...

...are expressions of a single system: organismic intelligence.

This chapter brings that system into view as a unified structure: the natural perceptual architecture humans are born with but not often taught to recognize.

When this structure is understood as a whole, the perception process stops feeling like a collection of techniques and becomes a continuous way of engaging reality.

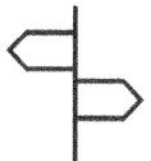

What Organismic Intelligence Actually Is

Organismic intelligence is the integrated perceptual system through which awareness operates. It includes:

> your perceptual-awareness interface
> your emotional tone
> your bodily and relational boundaries
> the space immediately around your body
> sensitivity to other people's presence and states
> sensitivity to environmental atmosphere
> symbolic and pattern-based informational processes
> temporal directionality and probability movement

These are not freestanding domains. They are differentiated functions within one continuous, self-organizing perceptual awareness system. You are registering all of them all the time, whether consciously or not. What changes with noticing them is not access, but discrimination, stability, and coordination.

The Five Core Perceptual Functions of Organismic Intelligence

The five perceptual functions described here have already appeared throughout earlier chapters in different ways. Here they are gathered into a single framework.

Organismic intelligence expresses itself through five primary functions. They are distinct yet constantly interacting.

1. Somatic Function: Sensation, posture, breath, nervous system regulation.

2. Emotional Function: Tone, affective resonance, emotional tone.

3. Relational–Energetic Function: Boundary clarity, interaction, coherence, spatial sensitivity.

4. Symbolic Function: Non-linear meaning, imagery, metaphor, pattern recognition.

5. Temporal Function: Directionality, momentum, approach, probability movement.

Each function contributes different information. Clarity comes from recognizing which function is active and allowing them to coordinate without collapse into story or reactivity.

1. The Somatic Function
The Foundation of Organismic Intelligence

The somatic function is your system's capacity to register and regulate information through physical sensation and nervous system activity.

This function includes:

> breath
> muscles
> nervous system activation
> heartbeat
> temperature
> pressure
> proprioception (the sense of where your body is in space and how it is moving)

Even indiscernible impressions often form here first, as micro-shifts in your body, before thought, emotion, or imagery appear.

You may notice this when a change in your posture, breath, or tension occurs before you can explain why.

This is why:

> knowing often feels physical
> timeline sensitivity begins as bodily change
> emotional sensing starts as texture
> symbolic impressions carry somatic tone

The body is not detached from perception.

It is the primary interface through which organismic intelligence receives, stabilizes, and grounds information.

Most perceptual errors occur when bodily signals are skipped or overridden.

Most perceptual clarity returns when your attention reconnects here.

The somatic function also helps regulate intensity.

When your awareness remains connected to your body, the process can encompass more without losing stability.

Pause. Check resonance.

Pause. Check resonance.

2. The Emotional Function
The Atmosphere Within the Body

The emotional function is your system's ability to register tonal information about situations, relationships, and environments through affective resonance.

This function includes:

> emotional frequencies
> affective tone
> mood shifts
> subtle affective resonance

You may notice this when a feeling tone appears in your body before you can explain it or attach a story to it.

At its clearest, emotion operates as tonal perception, not narrative.

It is records qualities such as:

> warm
> heavy
> open
> off

These are signals, not conclusions.

That distinction is extremely helpful because people often assume emotion explains why something is happening, when it actually indicates how something feels in your system.

When emotion remains at the level of tone, it adds sensitivity and nuance to what you perceive.

When it escalates into story, urgency, or personal meaning, it begins to distort what is being perceived.

Emotion, held cleanly, is not something to overcome.

It is one of your most precise instruments for reading relational and situational atmosphere.

3. The Relational-Energetic Function
Boundary, Coherence, & Interaction

The relational-energetic function is your system's capacity to register spatial and interpersonal dynamics through boundary awareness and relational sensing.

This function includes:

> extension of awareness beyond the physical body
> expansion and contraction
> boundary clarity
> interaction with others' presence
> coherence states

You may notice this when the atmosphere of a space or the presence of another person registers before any words are exchanged.

This is the level at which:

> you sense someone approaching before they speak
> you register presence behind you
> the tone of a room becomes immediately apparent
> interpersonal chemistry or resistance becomes tangible

The regional-energetic function structures perception across space and relationship.

It allows your system to record distance, proximity, overlap, and interaction without relying on sensory cues alone.

When boundaries are clear and perceptual coherence is stable, this function provides accurate relational information.

When boundaries are diffuse or your attention is entangled, information here becomes noisy or confusing.

Pause. Check resonance.

Pause. Check resonance.

4. The Symbolic Function
The Intellect's Language for Non-linear Perception

The symbolic function is your system's ability to represent complex or non-linear information through imagery, metaphor, and pattern.

This function includes:

⟩ images
⟩ metaphors
⟩ colors and shapes
⟩ archetypal tones
⟩ dream-like fragments
⟩ meaning-patterns

You may notice this when an image, metaphor, or fragment of meaning appears suddenly without a clear logical origin.

The symbolic function translates information that does not arrive as facts, sequences, or sensory data.

It allows complexity to appear in manageable form.

Symbols are not messages to believe.

They are provisional forms that meaning takes so it can be shaped without being forced into certainty.

When held lightly, symbols provide orientation and pattern recognition.

When taken literally or interpreted too quickly, they become a primary source of distortion.

The symbolic function acts as a bridge between deeper perceptual processes and conscious understanding: useful, powerful, and dependent on grounding and restraint.

91

5. The Temporal Function
Sensitivity to Movement Within Time

The temporal function is your system's capacity to register directional change and emerging probability within unfolding situations.

This function includes:

⟩ timeline signals
⟩ probability currents
⟩ pre-sensory activation
⟩ pre-emotional shifts
⟩ directional sense
⟩ momentum and approach

You may notice this when a situation begins to feel as though it is moving toward or away from something before any visible outcome appears.

The temporal function registers how situations are leaning, gathering, or dissolving before outcomes become visible.

It does not reveal fixed futures.

It detects movement already underway: changes in probability, direction, and momentum as they begin to organize in the present.

This is timeline sensitivity as lived experience. It is not prediction, but sensitivity to time in motion.

Information arrives as direction rather than detail, tendency rather than certainty.

When held with neutrality and grounding, the temporal function supports timely response without urgency.

When interpreted prematurely, it collapses into anxiety or narrative.

Pause. Check resonance.

How the Functions Interact

The functions of organismic intelligence are not stacked like floors or activated one at a time.

They interweave continuously.

A single experience may register across several functions almost simultaneously.

For example:

> a sinking sensation in the body (somatic)
> a shift toward unease or heaviness (emotional)
> a subtle contraction in the perceptual boundary (energetic)
> an image or fragment such as broken glass (symbolic)
> a sense of approach or impending disruption (temporal)

No single function causes the others.

Each reflects the same information as it takes form across different perceptual contexts.

What you notice first may vary.

> Sometimes your body registers before imagery appears.
> Sometimes a symbol arises before emotion becomes clear.
> Sometimes direction is sensed before sensation.

Understanding this interweaving prevents two common errors:

1. Treating one impression as more "true" than the others.
2. Interpreting any single impression in isolation.

Clarity emerges not by isolating functions, but by recognizing how they move as one coordinated process.

Three Organizing Patterns of Organismic Intelligence

These are not rules imposed on perception. They are recurring patterns that become visible when perception is observed carefully over time.

Pattern 1: Perception Registers as a Cascade

Perceptual information often registers across multiple functions in a loose sequence, sometimes in milliseconds, sometimes over longer spans:

〉   symbol / pattern → tone → body → conscious recognition

An impression may enter through any function first. A symbol might appear before sensation. A bodily shift may precede emotion or imagery.

What tends to happen, regardless of entry point, is stabilization through the body.

Often, you have already perceived something before you consciously recognize that perception has occurred. This is why a sense of something can feel instantaneous, vague, or "already known" before you can name it.

Pattern 2: Meaning Clarifies When Interpretation Moves Ground-Up

When making sense of an impression, clarity increases when interpretation proceeds in the opposite direction of arrival:

〉   body → tone → relational response → symbol → temporal direction

Beginning with what is most concrete (sensation, tone, and relational response) reduces distortion.

Symbols and timeline impressions become clearer when they are grounded in somatic and emotional data rather than interpreted on their own.

This is not a rule, but a practical orientation: meaning tends to stabilize when it is anchored in what is least malleable.

Pattern 3: Stability Shapes Accuracy

Perceptual coherence is strongly influenced by the overall stability of your system.

Two conditions are especially influential:

1. Embodied stability: grounding, boundary integrity, and consistency.
2. Emotional neutrality: low urgency, low reactivity, not emotional suppression.

When these are present, information tends to be more proportionate, more stable, and more reliable.

When they are absent, signals are more likely to blur, inflate, or fragment into noise.

Stability does not create perception. It determines how clearly raw data can be recorded and held above the noise.

Pause. Check resonance.

The Four Modes of Unified Perception

When the functions of organismic intelligence operate in coordination, four perceptual modes tend to emerge naturally. These are not special states to achieve, but stable ways your system organizes when it is clear and well-regulated.

1. **Embodied Awareness**
   Sensing through your body with clarity and presence, without dissociation or overload.

2. **Emotional Intelligence**
   Reading emotional tone / frequency without collapsing into narrative, reactivity, or projection.

3. **Relational-Environmental Intelligence**
   Sensing presence, atmosphere, and interaction (between people and within places) without merging or confusion.

4. **Symbolic-Temporal Insight**
   Recognizing patterns, meaning, and directional movement without literalism, urgency, or distortion.

When these modes are active together, the process feels less like an effort and more like a natural, continuous orientation to life.

Integrated Navigation: The Organismic Loop

In Exploration 20.4, this sequence was introduced as a repeatable way of staying oriented when multiple perceptual contexts are active at once. Rather than a technique to perform, it describes a recurring pattern your system already uses when perception remains coherent. You can return to this loop whenever experience becomes complex or overwhelming.

1. Orient. Briefly recognize your vantage point of awareness before engaging with the experience.

2. Attune. Notice the signal as it registers:
   body → emotion → relational response → symbol → temporal direction

3. Anchor. Return to stability through:
   breath → posture → boundary

4. Differentiate. Recognize which perceptual context is active:
   personal → relational → environmental → deep

5. Interpret. Allow meaning to organize through:
   movement → tone → symbol → meaning

6. Withdraw and Reset. Release the connection and return to baseline: boundary → breath → coherence

This loop is not meant to be followed rigidly. It describes how organismic intelligence maintains orientation and clarity while moving through layered experience.

What you have been building throughout this book is not simply a collection of perceptual skills, but a way of remaining oriented (internally and externally) while life unfolds.

Pause. Check resonance.

EXPLORATION 21.1: Sequential Integration Scan
Experiencing Perception as a Coherent System

Objective

To sequentially differentiate perceptual functions while recognizing them as expressions of one continuous process.

Setup

Sit in a stable posture. Allow your breath to find its own rhythm.

Steps

1. Let your attention rest briefly with each perceptual function, one at a time:
    → somatic (body sensation, posture, breath)
    → emotional (tone, mood, affective quality)
    → energetic (boundary, expansion, contraction, spatial sense)
    → symbolic (images, metaphors, meaning-fragments, pattern)
    → temporal (direction, momentum, sense of approach or pause)
2. Spend a few moments with each, without trying to amplify or suppress anything.
3. Allow your attention to move naturally between them rather than forcing separation.

What to Watch For

⟩   variations in texture or quality rather than clearly bounded "states"
⟩   your attention moving fluidly between functions
⟩   moments where multiple functions seem active at once
⟩   occasions when data / signal appears to register first through bodily sensation

Reflection

↺   Which function did you notice most readily?
↺   Which felt less familiar?
↺   What did you notice about how your attention shifted as you moved through the scan?

What you're noticing.

EXPLORATION 21.2: Differentiated Meaning Formation
The Organization of Meaning Across Perceptual Functions

Objective

To notice how clarity increases when perceptual functions are distinguished before meaning forms.

Setup

Adopt a supported posture. Allow your breathing to regulate itself.

Steps

1. Bring to mind a recent impression or moment of knowing.
2. Note each of the following, without analysis:
     → bodily sensation (pressure, warmth, movement, posture)
     → emotional tone (neutral, heavy, light, unsettled, calm)
     → field response (expansion, contraction, steadiness, pull)
     → symbolic form (if present)
     → temporal direction (approach, pause, shift, release)
3. Let each form on its own before allowing them to recombine.

What to Watch For

⟩ increased clarity when functions are distinguished
⟩ urgency softening as tone and movement are identified
⟩ symbols becoming less compelling when separated from story
⟩ meaning organizing itself more simply than expected

Reflection

↺ What shifted when you distinguished between functions rather than interpreting all at once?
↺ Did anything change when narrative was set aside, even briefly?
↺ Which perceptual function appeared first, and which followed?
↺ Did separating sensation, tone, and movement affect how certain the meaning felt?
↺ When the elements recombined, did the meaning remain the same or reorganize itself?
↺ What function seemed most reliable in this moment?

What you're noticing.

EXPLORATION 21.3: Whole-Context Awareness

Multiple Perceptual Functions at Once

Objective

To sustain awareness of multiple perceptual functions simultaneously without losing your orientation.

Setup

Sit comfortably. Let your breath move without adjustment.

Steps

1. Let your attention include the following, without trying to organize or explain them:
    → your body (sensation, posture, breath)
    → your emotional tone (if any)
    → your perceptual boundary or field
    → the surrounding space or room
    → any symbolic or meaning-toned undercurrent
    → any sense of movement, direction, or lean
2. Allow these to be present together, without prioritizing one over another.
3. If your attention narrows, gently expand it again without effort.

What to Watch For

⟩ what you are aware of expanding without strain
⟩ multiple perceptual functions registering at once without competition
⟩ a reduced impulse to label, analyze, or explain
⟩ what you perceive feeling steadier or more spacious

Reflection

↺ What did you notice about how these functions coexisted? Did they feel layered, blended, or coordinated?

↺ Was there a particular anchor (body, breath, boundary, tone) that stabilized attention?

↺ When interpretation was set aside, what remained (movement, quality, timing, neutrality)?

What you're noticing.

Integration Practice 21
The Daily Unified Awareness Check

Once or twice a day, pause briefly and notice:

1. What is registering in my body right now?
2. What is the general emotional tone, if any?
3. How does my perceptual boundary feel in this moment?
4. Are symbolic or meaning-toned impressions present, or absent?
5. Is there any sense of movement, pause, or temporal direction?

This practice supports noticing your organismic intelligence is already operating as a whole system, without requiring interpretation or effort.

Observations.

Closing Thought

Your organismic intelligence is a lived structure.

It is how your system actually functions when it is coherent, grounded, and intact.

You now have direct experience of:

> how sensation becomes meaning
> how emotion informs perception
> how perceptual contexts interact
> how time registers as movement
> how these functions integrate into one coherent system

This is what Ingo recognized: humans are built for operational, multidimensional perception.

No new faculty was required.

What was needed was recognition of the structure already in place.

You now know that the architecture organizing your experience has been there all along.

CODA

PERCEPTUAL MATURITY

Opening Invitation

You have not arrived at a destination. You have arrived at a way of moving.

You began to recognize that information does not arrive through a single channel, but through a coordinated system (body, emotion, boundary, symbol, and timing) each registering a different aspect of the same unfolding reality.

Along the way, you discovered that clarity does not come from amplifying what you sense, but from organizing it: not to monitor experience, but to move through life while remaining oriented as it unfolds.

Your Reality Is a Map, Not the World Itself

Earlier in this series, perception itself was the focus:

- discovering how to notice
- discovering how to stabilize
- discovering how to differentiate signal from distortion

In this book, the emphasis shifted.

The question became:

How does perception function when it is lived from?

The answer was not a method. It was navigation.

You experienced how to:

- remain grounded in your personal context
- sense relational space without merging
- register environmental tone without confusion
- allow deeper-pattern information without inflation
- regulate exchange through selective permeability
- maintain your orientation so your awareness does not collapse into experience

Together, these processes allow what you perceive to remain usable.

Orientation Is the Throughline

What ultimately stabilizes your system is not effort, discipline, or vigilance.

It is orientation.

Holding orientation allows:

> emotion to move without becoming identity
> symbols to inform without becoming belief
> relational influence to register without displacing center
> complexity to be sensed without overwhelm

From this vantage point, the perceptual process does not demand action, certainty, or interpretation.

It offers information in proportion to what your system can hold.

This is perceptual maturity: not knowing more but being able to remain present with more.

The Quiet Shift

If something subtle has changed as you moved through this book, it may not feel dramatic.

You may notice:

> urgency appearing later, or not at all
> confusion resolving more quickly
> boundaries reasserting themselves without force
> meaning forming more slowly, and more reliably
> orientation returning without effort

These are signs that navigation is becoming implicit. Your system is doing what it was designed to do.

Nothing to Maintain

There is nothing here you need to hold onto.

If clarity fades, return to your:

> body
> breath
> boundary
> vantage point

Orientation restores itself when attention is allowed to settle.

Organismic perception organizes itself when it is not forced.

Living It

To live with organismic intelligence is not to consult it constantly. It is to trust that it is already in use.

1. You move.
2. You relate.
3. You decide.
4. You sense.
5. You disengage.
6. You reset.

All of this happens while you remain present but not absorbed.

The Pivot into Book Five

Up to now, the question has been:

How do I live from my organismic intelligence?

What follows asks:

How do I live from this orientation when it meets structure?

These forces do not appear as experiences inside you. They shape the conditions under which experience is allowed to register at all.

This is where perception stops being something you manage and becomes something you must hold within a larger world.

This is a different terrain.

Closing Thought

You are no longer noticing how perception works. You are navigating through how to live from it.

From here, active awareness and organismic perception do not need to expand further. They needs to remain held.

And when they are held, life becomes navigable... not because it is simpler, but because you are no longer lost inside it.

APPENDIX

Quick Reset Practices

The brief resets below are not techniques to master or practices to perform regularly. They are simple ways of returning your system to a workable state when it drifts, intensifies, or becomes unclear.

You may use them as needed, or not at all.

Body Reset
(returning to physical presence)

> Exhale longer than you inhale.
> Relax your shoulders.
> Feel a connection to the ground through your feet or seat.
> Drop into the present moment.

Boundary Reset
(restoring perceptual containment)

> Inhale → gently gather your attention to your perimeter.
> Exhale → allow your boundary to close.
> Focus on a soft containment around the body.

Coherence Reset
(stabilizing rhythm and tone)

> Inhale for 5 seconds.
> Exhale for 5 seconds.
> Bring to mind something you appreciate.
> Let your attention smooth and stabilize.

Emotional Check-In
(staying oriented with feeling)

> Where is the sensation located?
> What is its texture?
> What is its direction (up / down / inward / outward)?
> Can it soften with one breath?

Perceptual Reorientation
(returning to balanced attention)

> Turn your attention inward.
> Soften your visual focus.
> Allow your awareness to include the room around you.

SELECTED SCIENTIFIC & PHILOSOPHICAL FOUNDATIONS

The following works have informed the biological, cognitive, relational, and phenomenological perspectives that shape this book.

They are not cited exhaustively, but represent foundational contributions in self-regulation, meta-awareness, predictive processing, interoception, relational neuroscience, attentional control, boundary formation and perceptual integration.

The explorations in this book draw upon established findings in neurovisceral integration, executive control, salience detection, emotional regulation, embodied cognition, interpersonal attunement, and meta-conscious monitoring.

They are phenomenological practices (structured observations of lived experience) grounded in contemporary neuroscience and cognitive science.

References

Barrett, L. F. (2017). *How emotions are made: The secret life of the brain.* Houghton Mifflin Harcourt.

Blanke, O., & Metzinger, T. (2009). Full-body illusions and minimal phenomenal selfhood. *Trends in Cognitive Sciences, 13*(1), 7–13.

Clark, A. (2016). *Surfing uncertainty: Prediction, action, and the embodied mind.* Oxford University Press.

Craig, A. D. (2002). How do you feel? Interoception: The sense of the physiological condition of the body. *Nature Reviews Neuroscience, 3*(8), 655–666.

Critchley, H. D., & Garfinkel, S. N. (2017). Interoception and emotion. *Current Opinion in Psychology, 17,* 7–14.

Damasio, A. (1996). The somatic marker hypothesis and the possible functions of the prefrontal cortex. *Philosophical Transactions of the Royal Society B, 351*(1346), 1413–1420.

Damasio, A. (2010). *Self comes to mind: Constructing the conscious brain.* Pantheon Books.

Decety, J., & Jackson, P. L. (2004). The functional architecture of human empathy. *Behavioral and Cognitive Neuroscience Reviews, 3*(2), 71–100.

Farb, N. A. S., Segal, Z. V., Mayberg, H., Bean, J., McKeon, D., Fatima, Z., & Anderson, A. K. (2007). Attending to the present: Mindfulness meditation reveals distinct neural modes of self-reference. *Social Cognitive and Affective Neuroscience, 2*(4), 313–322.

Feldman, R. (2012). Parent–infant synchrony: A biobehavioral model of mutual influences in the formation of affiliative bonds. *Monographs of the Society for Research in Child Development, 77*(2), 42–51.

Friston, K. (2010). The free-energy principle: A unified brain theory? *Nature Reviews Neuroscience, 11*(2), 127–138.

Fonagy, P., & Target, M. (1997). Attachment and reflective function: Their role in self-organization. *Development and Psychopathology, 9*(4), 679–700.

Gross, J. J. (1998). The emerging field of emotion regulation: An integrative review. *Review of General Psychology, 2*(3), 271–299.

Hayes, S. C., Strosahl, K. D., & Wilson, K. G. (2012). *Acceptance and commitment therapy: The process and practice of mindful change* (2nd ed.). Guilford Press.

Hohwy, J. (2013). *The predictive mind.* Oxford University Press.

Holmes, E. A., Brown, R. J., Mansell, W., Fearon, R. P., Hunter, E. C., Frasquilho, F., & Oakley, D. A. (2005). Are there two qualitatively distinct forms of dissociation? A review and some clinical implications. *Clinical Psychology Review, 25*(1), 1–23.

Kabat-Zinn, J. (1990). *Full catastrophe living.* Delacorte.

Kross, E., & Ayduk, O. (2011). Making meaning out of negative experiences by self-distancing. *Current Directions in Psychological Science, 20*(3), 187–191.

Lutz, A., Dunne, J. D., & Davidson, R. J. (2007). Meditation and the neuroscience of consciousness. In P. Zelazo, M. Moscovitch, & E. Thompson (Eds.), *The Cambridge handbook of consciousness* (pp. 499–554). Cambridge University Press.

Merleau-Ponty, M. (2012). *Phenomenology of perception* (D. A. Landes, Trans.). Routledge. (Original work published 1945)

Metzinger, T. (2009). *The ego tunnel: The science of the mind and the myth of the self.* Basic Books.

Ogden, P., Minton, K., & Pain, C. (2006). *Trauma and the body: A sensorimotor approach to psychotherapy.* W. W. Norton.

Palumbo, R. V., et al. (2017). Interpersonal autonomic physiology: A systematic review. *Personality and Social Psychology Review, 21*(2), 99–141.

Porges, S. W. (2011). *The polyvagal theory.* W. W. Norton.

Posner, M. I., & Rothbart, M. K. (2007). Research on attention networks as a model for the integration of psychological science. *Annual Review of Psychology, 58*, 1–23.

Schooler, J. W. (2002). Re-representing consciousness: Dissociations between experience and meta-consciousness. *Trends in Cognitive Sciences, 6*(8), 339–344.

Schooler, J. W., et al. (2011). Meta-awareness, perceptual decoupling and the wandering mind. *Trends in Cognitive Sciences, 15*(7), 319–326.

Seeley, W. W., Menon, V., Schatzberg, A. F., Keller, J., Glover, G. H., Kenna, H., Reiss, A. L., & Greicius, M. D. (2007). Dissociable intrinsic connectivity networks for salience processing and executive control. *Journal of Neuroscience, 27*(9), 2349–2356.

Siegel, D. J. (2012). *The developing mind* (2nd ed.). Guilford Press.

Seth, A. (2021). *Being you: A new science of consciousness.* Dutton.

Sterling, P. (2012). Allostasis: A model of predictive regulation. *Physiology & Behavior, 106*(1), 5–15.

Swann, I. (1991). *Everybody's guide to natural ESP: Unlocking the extrasensory power of your mind.* Jeremy P. Tarcher.

Swann, I. (n.d.). *Dream files* [Unpublished materials]. Ingo Swann Papers, Special Collections, Irvine S. Ingram Library, University of West Georgia.

Teasdale, J. D., Segal, Z. V., Williams, J. M. G., Ridgeway, V. A., Soulsby, J. M., & Lau, M. A. (2002). Prevention of relapse/recurrence in major depression by mindfulness-based cognitive therapy. *Journal of Consulting and Clinical Psychology, 68*(4), 615–623.

Thayer, J. F., & Lane, R. D. (2000). A model of neurovisceral integration in emotion regulation. *Journal of Affective Disorders, 61*(3), 201–216.

Thompson, E. (2007). *Mind in life: Biology, phenomenology, and the sciences of mind.* Harvard University Press.

THE SERIES
You Are More Than You Think

Book One
What's Already There

Book Two
Where You Sit

Book Three
The Shape of Knowing

Book Four
Above the Noise

Book Five
The Gravity of Reality

Chapter numbers continue across volumes to reflect that the series unfolds as one integrated structure rather than as separate works. Each book stands on its own, but the numbering maintains the progression for readers who move across the entire sequence.

Elly Flippen is the niece of Ingo Swann and the editor of **Why Do We Feel There Is More to Us Than We, or Anyone, Knows About?**, as well as the author of **Conjunction.World**.

Her work is shaped by years of engagement with questions of perception, awareness, and the lived experience of human intelligence beyond habit and assumption.

She invites readers to rely on their own sensing and discernment, recognizing perception not as something to acquire, but as something already active and waiting to be understood.

To learn more about Ingo Swann and his work, visit **www.ingoswann.com.**